Corny Humor

More
Wit and Witticism

Large Type Edition

Published by

the National Federation

of the Blind

Table of Contents

Introduction

I truly believe the old adage, "when you laugh, the world laughs with you." Millions of Americans have enjoyed our WIT AND WITTICISM books and hardly a day goes by that someone doesn't write and thank me for helping to brighten their day.

I'm so glad to hear that because that's the whole purpose of our joke book series. Ever since I was first elected President of the National Federation of the Blind in 1986, I have included a funny or witty story, and a joke or two in the tape recording I send to be played for our members at their local monthly chapter meetings. I have done this because these "Presidential Messages" are always filled with the serious problems of blindness, and I want to share these jokes and funny stories with my friends...to take our minds off the problems of blindness and to lighten the day's burden with a little humor.

For years now, individuals from all over the country have been sending me jokes to share with others, and these jokes have been compiled into special books. This sixth edition of jokes and witty stories, CORNY HUMOR, MORE WIT AND WITTICISM, is due in large part to the many letters of thanks and encouragement we have received from people who have enjoyed reading our previous four editions.

I am pleased to present you with this all-new compilation of good humor and wit. I hope that in some small way this book will make your day better by making you smile and forget your daily problems...even for just a few minutes.

Marc Maurer
President

Why Large Type

The type size of this book is 14 point for two important reasons: One, because typesetting of 14 point or larger complies with federal standards for the printing of materials for visually impaired readers, and we want to show you exactly what type size is necessary for people with limited sight.

The second reason is that many of our friends and supporters have asked us to print our paperback books in 14 point type so they too can easily read them. Many people with limited sight do not use Braille. We hope that by printing this book in larger type than customary, many more people will be able to benefit from it.

Marc Maurer,
President

National Federation of the Blind

A Commentary on Culture

Did you hear about the part-time orchestra leader?

He was a semi-conductor.

Do you know MacAdam?

He's the first man in the Scottish Bible.

What relaxes a chess player?

Taking a knight off.

What grows on trees and is terrified of wolves?

The three little figs.

Why does a dressmaker
never lose her hooks?

Because she has an eye for
each of them.

Why did the hardware store
owner go to the psychiatrist?

He had a few loose screws.

And what is it to abdicate?

To give up on having a flat stomach.

Why do koala bears have pouches?

Because it's too hard to push a baby carriage up a tree!

What happened to the mechanic who fell asleep dreaming about mufflers?

He woke up exhausted.

Why do we call money bread?

Because everybody kneads it.

Mary: Did you leave a tip for the boy who delivers our newspapers?

Larry: Yes, dear. I put some of it in the bushes, some of it on the roof, and the rest of it in the front yard.

Knock, Knock

Knock, knock.

Who's there?

Carl.

Carl who?

Carl get you there faster
than a bike.

Knock, knock.

Who's there?

Dexter who?

Dexter Halls with boughs of holly.

Knock, knock.

Who's there?

Repeat.

Repeat who?

OK. Who, who, who, who.

Knock, knock.
Who's there?
Eddie.
Eddie who?
Eddie body home?

Knock, knock.

Who's there?

Allison.

Allison who?

Allison Wonderland.

Knock, knock.

Who's there?

Franz.

Franz who?

Franz, Romans, countrymen . . .

Knock, knock.

Who's there?

Dewey.

Dewey who?

Dewey have to do these

jokes all night?

Creatures Great and Small

What do you call a Tyrannosaurus Rex when it wears a cowboy hat and boots?

Tyrannosaurus Tex.

What do you give a sick bird?

Tweetment.

What kind of bird carries
the most weight?

A crane.

What do bees use to brush
their hair?

A honeycomb.

What did the 700 pound canary say?

"Here, Kitty, Kitty!"

Why was the fish afraid of the computer?

He didn't want to get caught in the internet!

What did the bee say to the flower?

What time do you open?

Why couldn't the leopard escape from the zoo?

He was always spotted.

What do ducks like with their soup?

Quackers.

Why can't you reach a zoo by telephone?

The lion's always busy.

What does a kitten become after it is three days old?

Four days old.

What do snakes do to end a fight?

They hiss and make up.

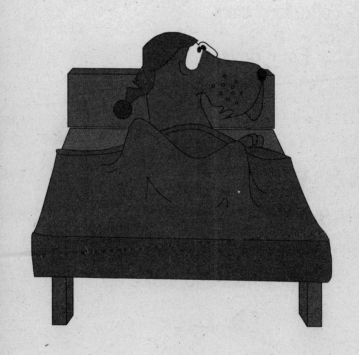

What do lazy dogs chase?

Parked cars.

What did one fish say to the other?

Keep your mouth shut and we won't get caught.

What's a frog's favorite drink?

Croak-a Cola.

Why is a spider so good at baseball?

Because it catches "flies."

What time is it when an elephant sits on a fence?

Time to get a new fence.

What do fish take to stay healthy?

Vitamin sea.

Riddles Galore

What is the largest pencil in the world?

Pennsylvania.

Where would you find an elephant?

It depends on where you lost him.

What instrument makes the most sour notes?

A pickle-o.

What can you hold in your right hand that you can't hold in your left?

Your left elbow.

When can't astronauts land on the moon?

When it's full.

What always flies but never rests?

The wind.

What's black and white and
a tiny bit of green?

Two zebras fighting over a
pickle.

Who holds up a school bus
with one hand?

A policeman.

What has one eye, but if it loses an eye becomes a nose?

Noise.

How do you spell Mississippi with one 'i'?

Cover one eye with your hand and spell it out.

What can be held without
ever being touched?

A conversation.

When is longhand quicker
than shorthand?

When it's on a clock.

Some Things Never Change

What do you get when you
drop a piano down a mine shaft?

A-flat minor.

Why did Miss Muffet need a
road map?

Because she lost her whey!

Why did the man wear a lot of clothing while painting?

The instructions read "Add three coats."

How does a boy fish communicate with a girl fish?

He drops her a line.

Did you hear the story about the pretty peacock?

No, but I heard it's a beautiful tale!

Did you hear about the sidewalk?

It's all over town.

Who was the greatest
financier in the Bible?

Noah, because he was
floating his stock while
everyone else was in liquidation.

Who was the greatest
comedian in the Bible?

Samson, because he brought
the house down.

Billy: I think my mom plans to straighten my room once and for all.

Roger: Why do you say that?

Billy: Because she's learning how to drive a bulldozer.

When is a shellfish stronger
than a shark?

When it's all mussel.

What is the least dangerous
kind of robbery?

A safe robbery.

When does a man have the right to scold his coffee?

When he has more than sufficient grounds.

Why can't a catfish be weighed?

Because it has no scales.

What do you call a camel with no hump?

Humphrey.

What do you get when you cross a tiger's path?

Eaten.

Real Signs from Around the World

At a towing company: "We don't charge an arm and a leg. We want tows."

On a plumber's van: "We repair what your husband fixed."

At an optometrist's office:
"If you don't see what you're
looking for, you've come to the
right place."

On an electrician's truck:
"Let us remove your shorts."

Sign on a fence: "Salesmen welcome. Dog food is expensive."

In a restaurant window: "Don't stand there and be hungry, come in and get fed up."

At a tire shop: "Invite us to your next blowout."

In a veterinarian's waiting room: "Be back in five minutes. Sit! Stay!"

In side a bowling alley: "Please be quiet, we need to hear a pin drop."

In the front yard of a funeral home: "Drive carefully. We'll wait."

Outside a muffler shop: "No appointment necessary, we hear you coming."

At a psychic's hotline: "Don't call us, we'll call you."

In a no smoking area: "If we see smoking we will assume you are on fire and take appropriate action."

At an exterminator's: Get rid of aunts. Zap does the job in 24 hours.

48

For Your Information

How did the farmer keep track of all his cattle?

With a cowculator.

What kind of dog does a scientist have?

A laboratory retriever.

Teacher: What is the first part of a geography book?

Alice: The table of continents.

What starts with a "T", is full of "T", and ends with "T"?.

A teapot.

Which moves faster, heat or cold?

Heat, because you can catch a cold.

Why should you never say "288" in polite conversation?

Because it's two gross!

What crackers are good at English?

Grammar crackers.

What do you call a whale with a large vocabulary?

Moby Dictionary.

What did the boy with the greatest mother do?

He built a mom-ument.

What do you call a maid with false teeth?

An indentured servant.

What does a one-eyed jack
o'lantern wear?

A pumpkin patch.

Where did Noah keep the
bees?

In the archives, of course.

What did the cow make
after the earthquake?

Milkshakes!

Where do sheep go
shopping?

At Woolworth's.

A Special Kind of Wisdom

Why is the man who invests all your money called a broker?

If horrific means horrible why doesn't terrific mean terrible?

Why do croutons come in airtight packages? They're stale bread to begin with.

Why is a person who plays piano a pianist, but a person who drives a car isn't a racist?

When someone asks you a penny for your thoughts and you put your two cents in, what happens to the other penny?

A baby-sitter is a teenager acting like an adult while the adults are out acting like teenagers.

If a lawyer is disbarred, a priest defrocked, can a cowboy be deranged, or a politician devoted?

How about a podiatrist defeated, or a detective dissolved?

King: You have offended me and I condemn you to death!

Fool: Death!

King: Yes, but since you have been a good fool, I will let you choose your manner of death.

Fool: I choose to die of old age.

If you can eat the same food every day and be grateful for it,

If you can understand when your loved ones are too busy to give you any time,

If you can take criticism and blame without resentment,

If you can resist treating a rich friend better than a poor one,

If you can face the world without lies and deceit,

If you can say honestly that deep in your heart you have no prejudice against creed, color or politics,

Then, my friend, you are almost as good as your dog.

Life in the Fast Lane

If someone with multiple personalities threatens to kill himself, is it considered a hostage situation?

One day a man answers his door and there's a snail at his doorstep. The man picks it up and tosses it into the garden.

Two years later, he hears a knock on his door. He opens the door and it's the same snail.

And the snail says, "Hey, what was that all about?"

Why is a calendar so popular?

Because it has lots of dates.

What kind of horse never wins a race?

A sawhorse.

Why did the man ruin his piano?

He was looking for his keys.

What did the valentine say to the postage stamp?

You send me!

What is the hardest thing about learning to roller skate?

The pavement.

How can you tell you've got a bad singer at your front door?

He can't find the key and he doesn't know when to come in.

What do you call a jacket
that goes up in flames?

A blazer.

What do people sing in their
bathtubs?

Soap operas.

Are there any colors you can actually touch?

Sure, haven't you ever felt blue?

What do you call a knife that cuts four loaves of bread at a time?

A four-loaf cleaver.

72

Culture Shock

A cowboy walks into a bar and orders a beer. His hat is made of brown wrapping paper, his shirt and vest are made of waxed paper, and his chaps, pants, and even his boots are made of paper.

Pretty soon they arrest him for rustling.

What's the difference between a magician and a psychologist?

A psychologist pulls a habit out of a rat.

What do you call a fairy that doesn't bathe?

Stinkerbell.

Did you hear about the labor negotiation in the book store?

They went into binding arbitration.

Two Eskimos sitting in a kayak were chilly. When they lit a fire in the craft it sank, proving once and for all that you can't have your kayak and heat it too.

What does a bee lumberjack use to cut down trees?

A buzz saw.

What does a boy monster do when a girl monster rolls her eyes at him?

He rolls them right back to her.

Where do mummies go when they're in Arizona?

The Petrified Forest.

What person is always hurrying?

A Russian.

Why do lighthouse keepers raise chickens?

So they can have eggs with their beacon.

What does the sun do when it sets?

Makes a night of it.

What is horse sense?

Just stable thinking.

What is a fast tricycle?

A tot rod.

Some friars were behind on their belfry payments so they opened a florist shop to raise money. They did so well that a rival florist in town thought the competition was unfair.

He petitioned the church to close down the shop, but they would not. He went to the city leaders, but they refused to get involved. He begged the friars themselves, but they ignored him.

Finally, the rival florist hired Hugh McTaggert, the roughest, meanest thug in town, who threatened the friars' lives if they didn't close the shop. Terrified, they did so, proving that...

Hugh, and only Hugh, can prevent florist friars.

Daffy Definitions

Forger: A man who's always ready to write a wrong.

Daily ice cream cone: Scoop du jour

Impeccable: debeaked hen

Russian canned fish:
Czardines

Artery: The study of
painting

Kindred: fear that relatives
are coming to stay

Pillow: Nap sack

Violin: a bad hotel

Politics: a parrot who
swallowed a watch

Atrophy: an award given to
those who don't exercise

Help Change What It Means To Be Blind By Taking These Actions

☑ Take time to learn what blind people are really like. Get to know one of us on a personal basis.

☑ Promote Braille literacy. Insist that blind children be taught Braille in the public schools. Blind children who can't read can't compete.

☑ Tell an employer that blind people can be good employees. Blind people face a 70% unemployment rate. You can help.

☑ Seek out parents of blind children. Help form a support group in your community. Informed parents give children opportunities.

☑ Distribute Kernel Books (stories about the capabilities of blind persons) to local public libraries and schools.

☑ Tell others the things you know about the capabilities of blind people and the help available to them-- friends, family members, employers, and community leaders. Understanding what blindness really means is the true key to solving the problems blind people face.

NATIONAL FEDERATION OF THE BLIND

We Care About You Too! If a friend or family member needs assistance with problems of blindness, please write: Marc Maurer, President, 1800 Johnson Street, Suite 300, Baltimore, Maryland 21230-4998.